DO TORNADOES REALLY TWIST?

Questions and Answers About
Tornadoes and Hurricanes

BY MELVIN AND GILDA BERGER
ILLUSTRATED BY HIGGINS BOND

SCHOLASTIC
REFERENCE

CONTENTS

KEY TO ABBREVIATIONS
cm = centimeter/centimetre
ha = hectare
km = kilometer/kilometre
km² = square kilometer/kilometre
kph = kilometers/kilometres per hour
mph = miles per hour
t = tonne
°C = degrees Celsius

Library of Congress Cataloging-in-Publication Data

Berger, Melvin.
   Do tornadoes really twist? : questions and answers about tornadoes and hurricanes / by Melvin Berger and Gilda Berger; illustrated by Barbara Higgins Bond.
      p.   cm.—(Scholastic question and answer series)
   Includes index.
   Summary: Provides answers to a variety of questions about tornadoes and hurricanes, including "Where do most tornadoes strike?" and "How long do hurricanes last?"
   [1. Tornadoes—Miscellanea—Juvenile literature.   2. Hurricanes—Miscellanea.
   3. Questions and Answers.]   I. Berger, Gilda.   II. Higgins Bond, Barbara.   III. Title.
   IV. Series: Berger, Melvin.   Scholastic question and answer series.
QC955.2.B47   2000   551.55′2—dc21   99-24946   CIP   AC

ISBN 0-439-09584-0 (pob); ISBN 0-439-14880-4 (pb)

Book design by David Saylor and Nancy Sabato

10 9 8 7 6 5 4 3 2 1   0/0 01 02 03 04

Printed in Mexico   49
First trade printing, November 2000

Expert Reader: Dr. Keith Seitter, American Meteorological Society, Boston, Massachusetts

For Judy Koppel, a treasured cousin
and an outstanding teacher
— M. AND G. BERGER

To my youngest sister, Cynthia Higgins-Owsinski, M.D.,
a brilliant and dynamic young woman
who is taking the world by storm
— HIGGINS BOND

INTRODUCTION

Tornadoes and hurricanes are among the most violent and terrifying of all natural events. No one who has lived through them ever forgets the strength and fury of these storms.

Perhaps you've been caught in a tornado or hurricane. Or you may have seen pictures on television or read about them. Either way, you probably have lots of questions. Do you wonder:

How these storms start?

When and where they strike?

How much damage they do?

Whether people can stop a tornado?

Which was the worst hurricane in history?

What you should do during a tornado or hurricane?

Do Tornadoes Really Twist? answers all these questions—and many, many more. It also gives lots of information and weird facts you can use to astound and amaze your friends.

So what are you waiting for? Turn the page and enter the scary world of tornadoes and hurricanes!

Melvin Berger   Gilda Berger

TORNADOES: WHAT AND WHY

Do tornadoes really twist?

Yes. At the center of the storm, tornado winds spin around at very high speeds. Some twist and twirl at more than 300 miles (480 km) an hour! Tornado winds are the hardest blowing winds on Earth. Small wonder that tornadoes are called twisters!

What is a tornado?

A severe windstorm. You know it's a tornado when you spot a twisting, spinning funnel reaching down from a huge dark cloud. The funnel looks like a huge elephant trunk swaying back and forth. A tornado funnel can be 10 feet (3 m) to slightly over 1 mile (1.6 km) wide.

Some funnels do not extend to the earth. Others touch down and race across land. Still others skip or leap from one point to another. They touch down, plow a path of destruction, and rise up into the air.

What color are tornado funnels?

Most are white or clear in color at first. They may even seem to shimmer in the light. When they touch the ground, however, the funnels turn black or dark gray as they sweep up tons of dirt, dust, and debris.

What happens before a tornado?

A severe thunderstorm strikes the area. Very few thunderstorms produce tornadoes. But every tornado is formed by a parent thunderstorm.

This diagram shows tornado winds
twisting counterclockwise.

Do hailstones fall before a tornado?

Quite often. The strong thunderstorms that create tornadoes often produce hailstones as well.

Hailstones form when winds carry raindrops up to where it is very cold. The raindrops freeze and become bits of ice. The icy lumps start to fall and collide with drops of water in the clouds. The water freezes onto the icy bits, making them grow larger. This happens again and again until the icy lumps are big and heavy. Then they fall to the earth as hailstones.

How do tornadoes grow out of thunderstorms?

No one is quite sure. Scientists have several theories about how tornadoes form and are working hard to understand them better. Some severe thunderstorms produce the powerful, twisting winds of a tornado. But most thunderstorms do not and scientists are trying to find out why.

Do tornado winds always twist in the same direction?

No. In the Northern Hemisphere, most tornadoes twist counterclockwise. In the Southern Hemisphere, most twist clockwise.

How big are tornadoes?

Not big at all. Tornadoes are usually less than 1 mile (1.6 km) wide and travel along paths that are no more than 16 miles (26 km) long. Tornadoes may be small, but their power and violence cause great devastation.

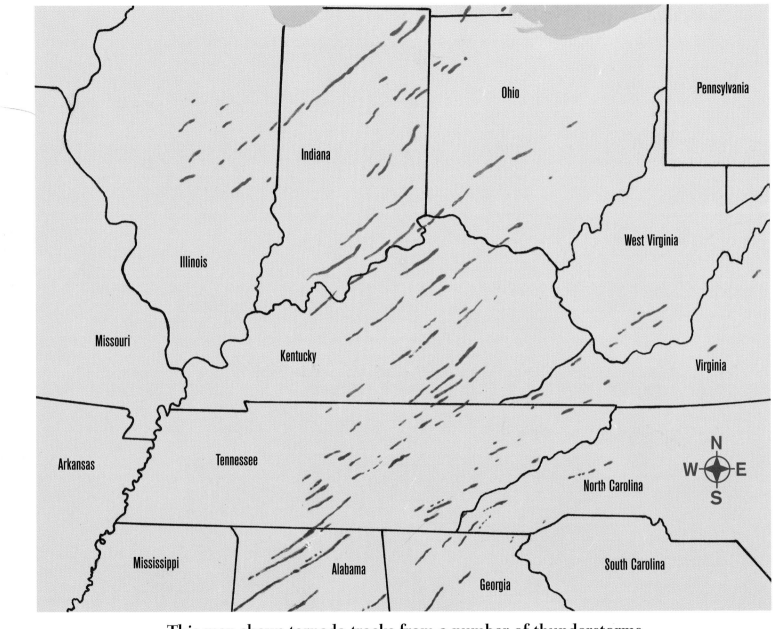

This map shows tornado tracks from a number of thunderstorms
that occurred on April 3 and 4 of 1974.

How long do tornadoes last?

Usually less than one hour. Some tornadoes die out in just a few minutes.

Groups of tornadoes sometimes form at about the same time. These tornadoes strike one after another, creating stormy conditions for several hours.

In which direction do tornadoes move?

In the United States, most move from the southwest to the northeast. This is because tornadoes travel with their parent thunderstorms, which usually go in this direction.

Weather experts map the movement of tornadoes by marking the tracks tornadoes leave when they touch the earth.

How fast do tornadoes move?

About 35 miles (56 km) an hour. The most dangerous ones reach speeds as high as 70 miles (113 km) an hour! The fastest-moving tornado on record occurred on March 18, 1925. The storm passed through the middle of the United States at the speed of a freight train—up to 73 miles (117 km) an hour!

Do tornadoes make noise?

Yes. The powerful spinning funnel wind often makes a shrill hissing or whistling noise that you can hear for miles around. Some say the sound is like the buzzing of a million bees.

When the tornado touches down and rips across the earth, the sound changes. The hiss becomes a loud, deafening roar. People compare it to the noise of 100 jumbo jets taking off at the same time! Others say it is more like the sound of a speeding train rumbling through a narrow tunnel. Either way, the noise of a tornado is not one that you would soon forget!

Do tornadoes make houses explode?

No. In the past scientists thought tornadoes created a vacuum that made houses explode. But now they know that's not true. Houses often just seem to have exploded because the strong winds blow off their roofs and walls.

How much damage do tornadoes cause?

Plenty. The powerful twisting winds of a tornado can pick up objects as big as trains, carry them aloft, and then smash them down on the ground. Do you remember the tornado in *The Wizard of Oz*? The storm comes to Kansas, picks up Dorothy's house, and carries it far, far away to the magical land of Oz! That was just a movie, but tornadoes have lifted whole houses off their foundations and moved them many feet (meters) away.

Tornado damage stays within a narrow path. A house on one side of a street may be smashed to bits. A house on the other side will often not even have one broken window.

Are tornadoes always violent?

Yes. But sometimes the tornado's winds lift up objects and then set them down safely. One tornado picked up a crate of eggs, carried it 500 yards (457 m), and placed it on the ground without cracking a single shell! Another tornado near Ancona, Italy, in September 1981 hoisted a carriage with a sleeping baby 50 feet (15 m) into the air. It then set the carriage down nearly 330 feet (101 m) away—without even waking the child!

What happens when a tornado passes over water?

You get a waterspout. Instead of pulling up dirt and debris, the tornado pulls up water. Most waterspouts last about a half hour. The funnel winds spin more slowly over water than over land.

Waterspout

TORNADOES: WHEN AND WHERE

When do tornadoes occur?

All year long. But most tornadoes come between April and June, with the highest number in May. The fewest occur during December and January.

Tornadoes can form at any time of day or night. But most develop late in the afternoon, the warmest time of the day. The largest number touch down between 4 and 6 P.M.

Where do most tornadoes strike?

The midsection of the United States and Canada. But every state of the United States, including Alaska and Hawaii, has had at least one tornado.

The record for most tornadoes in the United States was set in April 1974. During one 24-hour period, 148 tornadoes slammed through the South and Midwest!

What is Tornado Alley?

A stretch of land in the middle of the United States. Tornado Alley includes parts of Texas, Oklahoma, Kansas, Missouri, Nebraska, Arkansas, Iowa, Alabama, Florida, and Mississippi. More tornadoes pass through this area than anywhere else in the world.

Thunderstorms form in Tornado Alley when cold air flowing across the Rocky Mountains meets warm air flowing up from the Gulf of Mexico. Only a few of the thousands of thunderstorms that form there produce tornadoes.

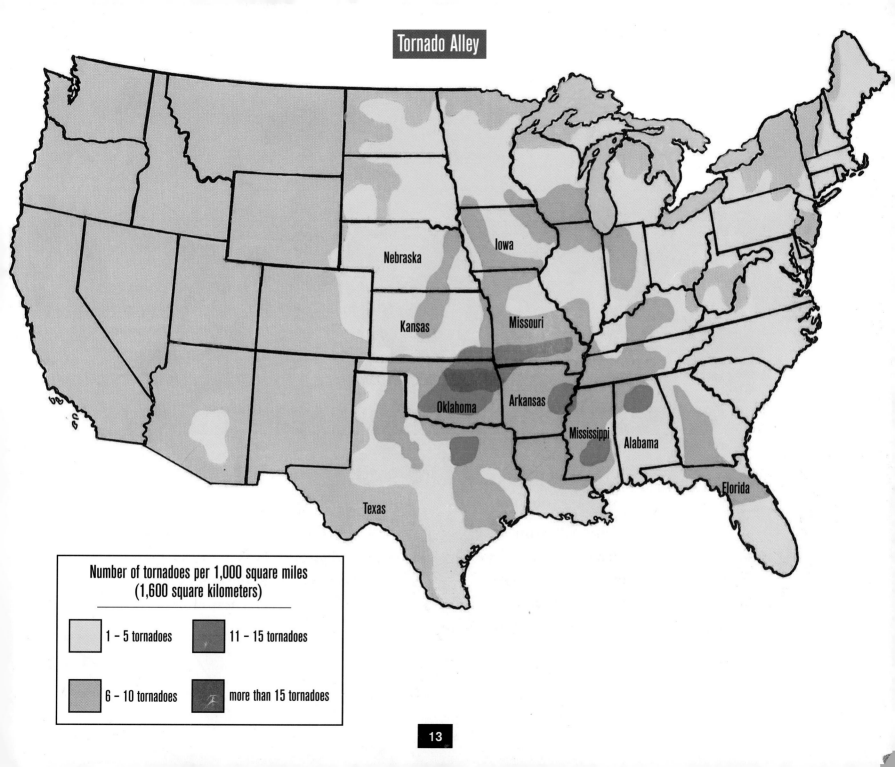

Tornado Alley

Nebraska

Iowa

Kansas

Missouri

Oklahoma

Arkansas

Mississippi

Alabama

Texas

Florida

**Number of tornadoes per 1,000 square miles
(1,600 square kilometers)**

- 1 – 5 tornadoes
- 11 – 15 tornadoes
- 6 – 10 tornadoes
- more than 15 tornadoes

A tornado approaches, 1925

How many tornadoes occur each year in the United States?

About 800. Because it is so huge, Texas has more tornadoes than any other state—an average of 139 a year. In 1967, and again in 1995, 232 twisters struck this state. But central Oklahoma is struck by tornadoes more often than anyplace else in the world.

Can mountains stop a tornado?

No. Every once in a while tornadoes do occur in mountainous country. A good example is the tornado that passed near Jackson, Wyoming, on July 21, 1987. The storm swept over mountains as high as 10,000 feet (3,048 m) without the winds losing their force.

Can tornadoes strike more than once in the same place?

They sure can. Two tornadoes hit the city of Austin, Texas, within a half hour on May 4, 1922. Oklahoma City has been struck 33 times in the last 90 years, making it the "Most Tornado-Battered City" in the entire country.

Which was the worst tornado of all time?

The tornado of March 18, 1925. This wild storm mostly moved in a straight line from Missouri to Indiana. Since it occurred long before the National Weather Service issued tornado watches and warnings, the storm caught many people off guard, without time to run for shelter.

Everything about the 1925 tornado was monstrous:

- Path—219 miles (352 km)
- Speed—as high as 73 miles (117 km) an hour
- Width—1 mile (1.6 km)
- Area of destruction—164 square miles (425 km²)
- Duration—3½ hours
- Number injured—2,027 people
- Number killed—689 people
- Cost—$17 million

Which tornado had the longest path?

The twister of May 26, 1917. This storm smashed a path 293 miles (471 km) long, from the town of Louisiana, Missouri, all the way to Jennings County, Indiana.

Which tornado almost wiped out a town?

The one that struck the small town of Coatesville, Indiana, population 500, on the evening of March 26, 1948. The destructive winds leveled four out of every five buildings, killed 16 people, and injured 150 more.

When did a series of tornadoes strike 13 states?

April 3–4, 1974. A cluster of 148 tornadoes struck parts of 13 states. Experts tell us the storm claimed 308 lives, sent 6,000 people to the hospital, and caused $600 million in damage. The number of injured soared because people did not pay attention to the tornado warnings and didn't know how to stay safe during the storm.

Which tornado took the most lives?

A tornado in the country of Bangladesh on April 26, 1989. The dreadful storm left 1,300 people dead.

How many die in tornadoes each year in the U.S.?

About 100 people. Between 1916 and 1953 the average yearly death toll in the United States was 230. In the years since then, as the warning system improved, the number has dropped substantially. By far, the worst single year was 1925 when 842 people lost their lives in tornadoes.

What are some unusual tornado facts?

The tornado of April 16, 1880, tore apart a house near Marshall, Missouri, and dropped the heavy timbers 12 miles (19 km) away.

The winds of the June 23, 1944, tornado blew all the water out of the West Fork River in West Virginia for a few minutes.

The tornado of June 10, 1958, sucked a woman out of a window in her El Dorado, Kansas, home. The winds carried her 60 feet (18 m) and gently dropped her to the ground. She landed in a pile of storm debris. Right next to her was a phonograph record of the song "Stormy Weather"!

Can trains survive tornadoes?

Not if they're in the path of a tornado. A powerful tornado struck a moving train near Moorhead, Minnesota, on May 27, 1931. The storm lifted an 83-ton (84.3 t) railroad car with 117 passengers off the tracks and dropped it in a ditch 80 feet (24 m) away.

A train carrying brand-new cars was passing through Ohio when a tornado hit. In just a few minutes, the tornado broke the windows of every single car.

Which tornado was the strangest of all?

The one that touched down in Great Bend, Kansas, in November 1915. The strong winds of this tornado

- blew a check to Palmyra, Nebraska—a full 305 miles (491 km) away—the farthest that a tornado has ever carried debris.
- picked up some 45,000 ducks and then rained them down to the earth.
- ripped off one wall of Grant Jones's grocery store, but didn't disturb the cans and boxes on the shelves against that wall.

Despite all that happened in Great Bend, farmers 2 miles (3 km) away knew nothing of the tornado!

Who studies tornadoes?

Weather scientists called meteorologists. From the ground, they track the parent thunderstorms of tornadoes with radar. Satellites follow the movement of the storms from high up in space. Meteorologists also launch planes and balloons into areas around a tornado to learn about the surrounding winds and weather conditions.

How do scientists rate tornadoes?

By the Fujita-Pearson, or F, scale. Scientists rate the weaker tornadoes F-0 or F-1. The most violent tornadoes, rated F-4 or F-5, do the most damage and cause the most deaths.

	WIND SPEED	DAMAGE
F-0	40–72 mph (64–116 kph)	Some signs blown down; tree branches broken.
F-1	73–112 mph (117–180 kph)	Trees snapped; windows shattered.
F-2	113–157 mph (181–253 kph)	Trees uprooted; building roofs torn off.
F-3	158–206 mph (254–332 kph)	Most trees overturned; building walls ripped away; trains wrecked.
F-4	207–260 mph (333–419 kph)	Big houses destroyed; cars thrown off road.
F-5	261–318 mph (420–512 kph)	Big houses carried long distances; cars tossed into the air.

Is any place safe from tornadoes?

No. No place, including rivers, lakes, and mountains, is safe from tornadoes.

Instruments are attached to
the weather balloon.

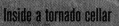
Inside a tornado cellar

What is a tornado watch?

A forecast from meteorologists at the Storm Prediction Center in Norman, Oklahoma, that a tornado is possible in your area. Meteorologists broadcast the news over radio and television. They tell listeners that a tornado may develop in the next few hours.

What is a tornado warning?

An alert issued by the local National Weather Service office that a tornado has been sighted or picked up by weather radar. A tornado warning lets you know a tornado's expected path and urges those at risk to seek shelter immediately.

What should you do outdoors in a tornado?

Run to the nearest tornado cellar. If this is not possible, lie flat in a ditch or low part of the ground. Cover your head with your hands. Remember that flying debris from tornadoes causes most deaths and injuries.

If you're in an automobile, get out right away. Do not try to outrun a tornado. Take shelter in a house or other building.

What should you do indoors in a tornado?

Move to an underground shelter, such as a basement. If no shelter is available, take cover in an inside closet, bathroom, or hallway on the lowest floor. You can also get under a mattress and cover your head with your hands.

Stay away from windows. The glass may shatter. Also, when there's thunder and lightning, avoid touching metal objects or exposed wires.

If you're in a mobile home, leave and take shelter in another building or a ditch. Tornadoes lift and wreck mobile homes as if they were made of paper.

HURRICANES: WHAT AND WHY

What is a hurricane?

A large, donut-shaped storm with heavy rain and strong winds blowing around a calm center. Hurricanes are the biggest and most destructive storms on Earth.

What is the difference between hurricanes and tornadoes?

Hurricanes are huge. Tornadoes are much smaller.

Hurricanes are made up of many thunderstorms and rain clouds with heavy rainfall. Tornadoes, on the other hand, are formed by one thunderstorm and have little rain.

Hurricanes form over warm ocean water. Most tornadoes form over land.

How are hurricanes like tornadoes?

Both have strong winds blowing around in circles rather than in straight lines.

Both usually keep moving.

And both have very strong updrafts that carry warm, moist air high up in the atmosphere.

What happens before a hurricane?

Winds blow hard and there is a lot of moisture in the air. The level of the sea rises and the waters get very rough. As the hurricane builds, the ocean rises dangerously high with huge waves, called ocean swells.

How is a hurricane born?

An area of low pressure forms over a tropical sea. The sun beats down and warms the water to at least 80 degrees Fahrenheit (27°C). This warms the air. It also adds lots of moisture to the air. The warm, moist air starts to rise.

The upward movement of the air soon forms a cluster of thunderstorms and rain clouds, with heavy rains and thunder and lightning. Sometimes these storms and clouds come together in a particular way—and a hurricane is born.

How does a hurricane develop?

Warm, moist air continues to rise. The updraft sucks in still more air. The rushing air starts to spin around in gigantic spiral winds. When the winds reach a speed of 39 miles (63 km) an hour, it's a tropical storm. Every year about 10 tropical storms form in seas off the coast of the United States.

In about 6 of every 10 tropical storms, the rainfall keeps getting heavier. At the same time, the spinning winds blow faster and harder. When winds reach 74 miles (119 km) an hour, the tropical storm becomes a hurricane.

How big are hurricanes?

Most are about 340 miles (550 km) across. The very largest hurricanes form in the Pacific Ocean. They may have diameters greater than 1,000 miles (1,600 km).

Hurricanes also extend way up above sea level. Monster hurricanes may reach as high as 10 miles (16 km) into the air.

How many hurricanes form every year?

Worldwide, about 45 hurricanes form in tropical seas. They usually move in curved paths westward and away from the equator until they reach cooler water and die out. An average of about 5 hurricanes form in the Atlantic Ocean every year.

Where does the word *hurricane* come from?

Probably from the Spanish word *huracan*. But there may be other sources. According to Guatemalan folklore, the god of stormy weather is Hunrakan, and the god of thunder and lightning is Hurakan. In Suriname, people use the word *hyroacan* to mean devil. Anyway you look at it, hurricane spells trouble.

How fast do hurricane winds blow?

At least 74 miles (119 km) an hour. In fact, a storm isn't called a hurricane until its winds reach this speed. Around the center of the hurricane the wind speed may reach speeds as high as 150 miles (241 km) an hour. Only the mighty winds of a tornado blow faster and harder.

In which directions do hurricane winds blow?

Counterclockwise in the Northern Hemisphere, clockwise in the Southern Hemisphere.

Do hurricanes stay in one spot?

No. Almost all Atlantic Ocean hurricanes work their way west and north. Often, the hurricanes' heavy winds and pouring rains crash down with great fury on Atlantic Ocean coastlines.

How long does it take for a hurricane to pass overhead?

Nearly 10 hours. For the first 4 hours or so, pounding rains and strong winds move through the area. The storm topples trees, destroys houses, wrecks cars, and tears down electrical lines. Pieces of debris shoot past like bullets.

Then, suddenly, the winds and rain stop while the calm center of the hurricane passes overhead. The peace may last from a few minutes to an hour or so. Then, the other part of the storm arrives. The winds are often as powerful as before, but blow from the opposite direction. It may be another 5 hours before the weather finally clears.

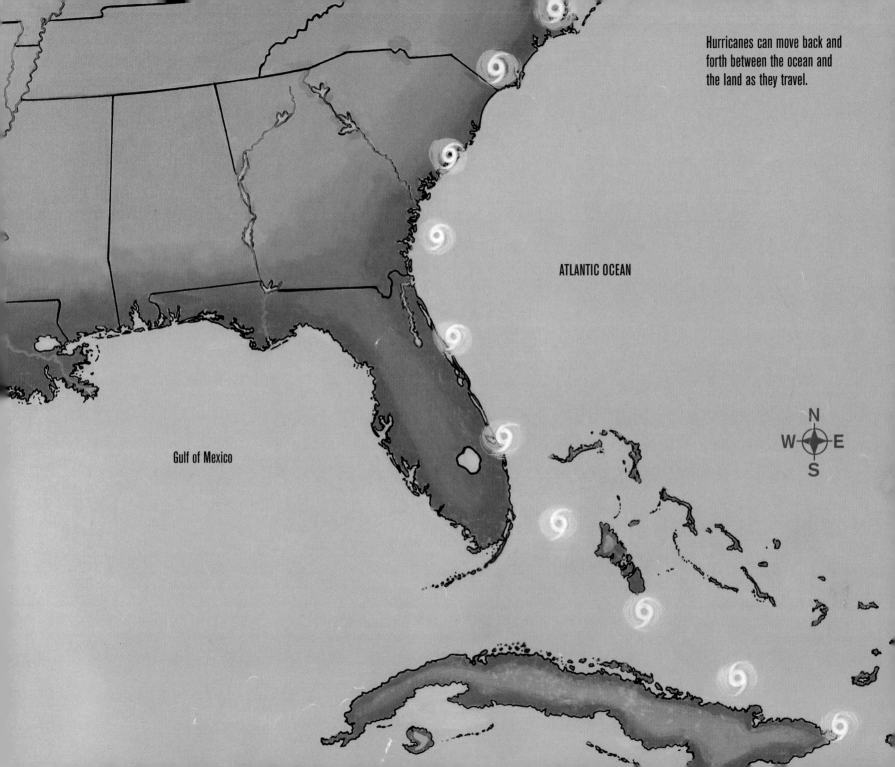

Hurricanes can move back and forth between the ocean and the land as they travel.

ATLANTIC OCEAN

Gulf of Mexico

N
W · E
S

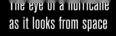

The eye of a hurricane
as it looks from space

What is the eye of a hurricane?

The calm center of the hurricane. On average the eye of a hurricane is about 14 miles (23 km) across. The eye, in a way, is like the hole in a giant donut surrounded by the extremely fast blowing winds of the hurricane. The eye shifts within the storm as the entire storm moves forward.

Why is the eye dangerous?

Because it tricks you into believing the storm is over. Some people go outdoors when the calm center passes overhead. Then, they may be injured or killed when the other half of the hurricane arrives.

But the eye can also be a blessing. Sailors often use the calm as a chance to tie their boats down before the rest of the storm moves in. And birds often fly safely in the eye of the hurricane.

How fast do hurricanes travel?

About 12 miles (19 km) an hour. In one day, a hurricane may cover about 300 miles (480 km). From space, the swirling clouds of a moving hurricane look much like a spinning top sliding over sea and land.

How long do hurricanes last?

About 10 days. The record is about a month. A hurricane starts to fade as it runs out of heat or moisture.

A hurricane moving over colder ocean waters cools off. Less rain starts to fall. When it passes over dry land, it loses its supply of moist air. The winds gradually slow down, even though the rainfall and flooding may continue. Soon the weather clears and the hurricane is over.

Do tornadoes and hurricanes ever occur together?

Yes, often. As many as one of every four hurricanes contains at least one tornado, and some hurricanes produce many tornadoes. In fact, the worst damage of Hurricane Andrew in August 1992 may have come from tornadoes within the hurricane. Even though tornadoes and hurricanes occur together, most of these tornadoes are weaker than those that form over the midwestern United States.

What are hurricane rain bands?

Spirals of thick, heavy clouds that unleash torrents of rain. Between the rain bands are light clouds that produce little or no rainfall.

Do hurricanes usually bring lightning?

Yes—mostly in the rain bands. The powerful winds, hard rains, and swirling clouds of a hurricane electrify the clouds. Giant sparks of electricity flash within a cloud, from one cloud to another, or from a cloud to the ground. We see these towering sparks as lightning.

How much rain falls from a hurricane?

Lots. The rain in a typical hurricane makes the water in a swimming pool rise about 9 inches (23 cm). But a big hurricane can dump as much as 20 inches (51 cm) over a given area. That's about half as much rain and snow as New York City gets in a whole year!

Hurricanes pick up enormous amounts of water vapor—about 2 billion tons (2.03 billion t) per day—from the oceans. High in the air, this water vapor turns to rain. When it falls it produces some of the world's heaviest rainfalls.

Which hurricane poured down the most rain?

The hurricane of March 15–16, 1952, at Cilaos, Reunion Island, in the Indian Ocean. Over 73 inches (185 cm) of rain fell.

The record rainfall in the U.S. occurred during Hurricane Dennis in 1981. Florida got a one-day soaking of 20 inches (51 cm)!

What is the danger of these huge amounts of rain?

Floods. Hurricane floods cause tremendous damage and loss of life. Also, their bad effects last long after the hurricane's rain and wind have stopped.

Hurricane Diane is an example. The storm lasted from August 7–21, 1955. It didn't do much harm when it first came ashore. But its heavy rainfall left vast areas of Pennsylvania, New York, and the New England states under water. The floods killed 200 people and caused some $700 million of damage.

What is a storm surge?

The sharp rise of ocean water due to a hurricane. When a storm hits, the sea may rise as high as 25 feet (8 m) above normal high tide.

Hurricane winds push on the water, piling it higher and higher, much like a snowplow pushing on a growing mound of snow. Also, the low pressure inside the hurricane pulls on the water, raising the level like water sucked up through a straw.

The highest storm surge on record occurred in Bathurst Bay, Australia, in 1899. The water rose to the height of a four-story building!

Are storm surges dangerous?

They sure are! Some experts say that 9 of every 10 people who die in hurricanes are killed by storm surges. Most drown. The huge, solid wall of water sweeps over beaches and other low-lying land areas. The surge washes away people—as well as buildings, trees, piers, and roads.

The floodwaters stay on land long after the hurricane passes. Since ocean water contains salt, many growing plants die. The salt and other chemicals left in the soil harm future crops and seep into wells and underground water supplies. This may make water unfit to drink for a long time.

Where do hurricanes get their names?

At first hurricanes were named after saints. Then, early in the twentieth century, an Australian meteorologist started to give hurricanes the names of people he didn't like. Around 1950, meteorologists began to use only female names. Since 1979, hurricane names follow the alphabet during each season, alternating between male and female names.

HURRICANES: WHEN AND WHERE

Where do most hurricanes form?

Over tropical oceans, usually within 1,000 miles (1,600 km) of the equator. They're called hurricanes when they form in the Atlantic Ocean, the Gulf of Mexico, or the Caribbean Sea. But those that form in the western part of the North Pacific Ocean near China and Japan are called typhoons. In the Bay of Bengal and the northern Indian Ocean people say they're cyclones. And in the Pacific Ocean around Australia the same storms have a funny name, willy-willies.

When is hurricane season?

From June through November in the Northern Hemisphere and from November through April in the Southern Hemisphere. During these months, the surface of the sea is at its warmest—about 80 to 86 degrees Fahrenheit (27 to 30°C).

Which hurricane stands out as one of the most powerful?

Hurricane Camille. This storm struck the Mississippi and Alabama coasts on August 17–18, 1969. Its winds blew a steady 200 miles (322 km) an hour with even stronger gusts. Storm surges of 25 feet (8 m) pounded the land, knocking over everything in their paths.

Which was the worst hurricane year?

The year 1955. Twelve major storms killed about 1,500 people and destroyed some $2 billion worth of property. The best year was 1983, with only four hurricanes.

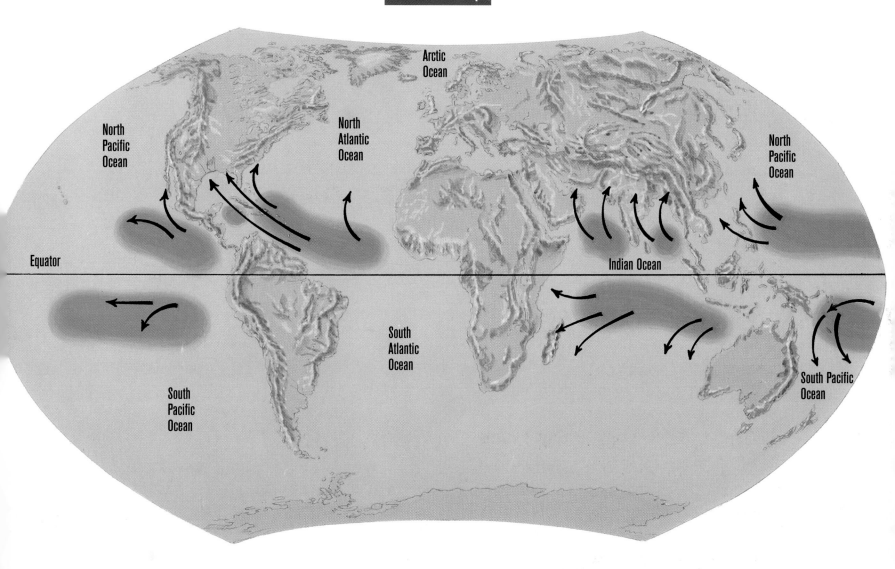

North Pacific Ocean

North Atlantic Ocean

Arctic Ocean

North Pacific Ocean

Equator

Indian Ocean

South Atlantic Ocean

South Pacific Ocean

South Pacific Ocean

The dark blue areas show where most hurricanes form.
The arrows show the directions the hurricanes travel.

Where do many of the worst hurricanes occur?

The Bay of Bengal and India. The land level is very low here and storm surges sweep over the coast. Millions of fishermen, farmers, and their families are in great danger whenever a cyclone heads their way. The city of Calcutta, with its millions of people, is often caught in the path of the floodwaters.

Which hurricane caused the worst loss of life?

The one that hit the Bay of Bengal on November 13, 1970. A 40-foot (12 m) storm surge plowed across the land, killing some 300,000 people.

In the United States, about 6,000 people died when a hurricane hit the city of Galveston, Texas, on September 8, 1900. But some experts disagree. They say the actual number is closer to 12,000!

Which hurricane helped start a new country?

The one that struck the Bay of Bengal in November 1970. Storm waters flooded 6,000 acres (2,428 ha), destroying many villages and killing thousands. The people blamed the government for not warning them of the storm and for taking too long to send help. Their fury led to a revolution. Within a few months, the people had formed a new country called Bangladesh.

Which United States hurricane caused the most damage?

Hurricane Andrew in August 1992. The storm wrecked 200,000 homes and businesses, left nearly 200,000 people homeless, and did over $30 billion in damage! The good news is the low death toll. Because of timely warnings, the storm killed only 53 people.

How do experts spot and track hurricanes?

With satellites and airplanes in the air, buoys and ships at sea, and radar and other equipment on land. Meteorologists follow all tropical storms that might become hurricanes.

Who are Hurricane Hunters?

People who fly planes into and around hurricanes. Hurricane Hunters measure the hurricane's energy, speed, and direction. They radio reports back to the National Hurricane Center (NHC) in Miami, Florida. Here, experts plot the hurricane's path, issue warnings, and forecast the path and strength of the storm.

What instruments do Hurricane Hunters use?

Radar and dropsondes. Radar bounces radio waves off the raindrops within the hurricane. The time it takes for the radio waves to get back to the radar shows the storm's size, position, speed, and direction.

Dropsondes are small packets of measuring instruments with tiny radio transmitters that hang from small parachutes. Hurricane Hunters drop them in and around the storm. As they fall, each dropsonde radios valuable information back to the plane.

How do meteorologists rate hurricanes?

By the Saffir-Simpson Hurricane Scale:

	WIND SPEED	SURGE HEIGHT
1	74–95 mph (119–153 kph)	4–5 feet (120–150 cm)
2	96–110 mph (154–177 kph)	6–8 feet (180–240 cm)
3	111–130 mph (178–209 kph)	9–12 feet (270–360 cm)
4	131–155 mph (210–249 kph)	13–18 feet (390–540 cm)
5	155+ mph (249+ kph)	18+ feet (540+ cm)

Hurricane Hunters

What is a hurricane watch?

A National Weather Service alert that a hurricane might reach land within two days. People should tune into radio or television to find out about the storm's progress.

What is a hurricane warning?

A National Weather Service alert that a hurricane is expected within 24 hours. People who live near the shore are usually told to go inland where it's safer.

How do people at sea get a hurricane warning?

Usually by radio or television. People on small boats near the coast may also see flag signals on shore. The signal for an approaching hurricane is two square red flags with black centers, one above the other. Two red lanterns with a white one in between give the same warning at night.

Is hurricane damage getting worse?

Yes. More people are moving to coastal areas, which is where hurricanes do the most damage. As this continues, more houses, cars, and roads are being wrecked by hurricanes.

Are hurricane injuries getting worse?

No. Every year, the scientists at the NHC get better at sending out warnings. With enough notice, people can either prepare for the storm or flee. The results are good. The number of people hurt or killed by hurricanes is going down.

What should you do before a hurricane?

Get out as soon as you're told to do so. But until then, or until the storm comes:
- Put tape crisscross on windows to prevent flying glass and put boards over big windows.
- Store water in bathtubs, pails, and bottles in case the water supply is cut off or polluted.
- Pick up toys, tools, flower pots, and other small objects outside the house. Store them in a safe place where they won't blow around and cause damage.
- Prepare a battery radio and a flashlight for use if the power goes off.

What should you do during a hurricane?

Stay indoors. Keep away from windows and follow the storm's progress on the radio.

Beware the eye of the hurricane. Don't let the calm trick you into thinking the storm is over. It isn't over until the second half of the hurricane passes by.

What should you do after the hurricane?

Stay out of disaster areas. Don't get in the way of first-aid and rescue workers.

Never touch a loose or dangling wire. A live electric wire can strike you down. Report dangerous situations like this to the police.

Do hurricanes do any good?

Yes. In spite of the destruction they cause, hurricanes help maintain the heat balance throughout the world. The heavy winds help carry heat from the tropics to the polar regions. Like a safety valve, hurricanes release excess energy and spread it out. Hurricane rains also bring lots of fresh water for crops and replenish groundwater.

INDEX

About the Authors

The Bergers live in the northeastern United States, where tornadoes rarely strike. They do travel quite a bit, however, and most recently experienced the powerful, twisting winds of a tornado on a trip to North Carolina.

About the Illustrator

Higgins Bond once lived in Arkansas, in the heart of Tornado Alley. She loves illustrating books about nature and science, and finds tornadoes fascinating.